Understanding Corporate Annual Reports

Fifth Edition

William R. Pasewark
Texas Tech University

 Irwin

Boston   Burr Ridge, IL   Dubuque, IA   Madison, WI   New York   San Francisco   St. Louis
Bangkok   Bogotá   Caracas   Kuala Lumpur   Lisbon   London   Madrid   Mexico City
Milan   Montreal   New Delhi   Santiago   Seoul   Singapore   Sydney   Taipei   Toronto

UNDERSTANDING CORPORATE ANNUAL REPORTS
William R. Pasewark

Published by McGraw-Hill/Irwin, an imprint of The McGraw-Hill Companies, Inc., 1221 Avenue of the Americas, New York, NY 10020. Copyright © 2004, 2000, 1998, 1995, 1994 by The McGraw-Hill Companies, Inc. All rights reserved.

1 2 3 4 5 6 7 8 9 0 BKM/BKM 0 9 8 7 6 5 4 3

ISBN 0-07-286821-X

www.mhhe.com

CONTENTS

PURPOSE OF THIS PROJECT

Communicating information to others is a fundamental human characteristic. Coaches use game statistics to plan strategies for future games. Teachers place grades on examinations so students may use the information to improve performance on future examinations. College graduates prepare resumes to describe their credentials to prospective employers.

You might say an annual report is a "resume" prepared for a corporation. Much of the information in corporate annual reports is dictated by generally accepted accounting principles (GAAP) and by the Securities and Exchange Commission (SEC), an agency of the federal government that regulates the trading of publicly-traded securities. For example, GAAP requires annual reports to disclose four financial statements: an income statement, a balance sheet, a statement of cash flows, and a statement of retained earnings, as well as a multitude of supplemental disclosures (ARB 43, Chapter 2A, Paragraph 2).

Annual reports communicate information between corporations and financial statement users. The primary purpose of an annual report is to convince existing stockholders to continue investing in the corporation. However, management may also use the annual report to:

- Persuade prospective stockholders to invest in the corporation.
- Inform security analysts about the investment qualities of the corporation.
- Inform lenders, such as bankers and suppliers, of the credit-worthiness of the corporation.
- Provide evidence to government agencies of compliance with regulations.

As a business student, you will probably use financial statements frequently in your profession. For example, as a manager or corporate strategist you may use financial statements to evaluate the performance of your own corporation, or your corporation's competitors. As a bank loan officer you may examine financial statements to decide whether to extend credit. If you become a corporate treasurer or fund manager you may use financial statements to choose between alternatives for your investment portfolio. Finally, as an individual investor you may use financial statements to select your personal investments.

The purpose of this project is to help you understand and analyze an annual report. When you complete the project, you will be very familiar with the corporation you analyzed. Later, you may use the analytical abilities gained in this project to analyze the financial statements of other corporations.

GETTING STARTED

Questions in this project are completed using the most recent annual financial data of a corporation. This data can be obtained in the following formats:

- hard copy annual report to stockholders from the corporation.
- hard copy of Form 10-K to the SEC from the corporation.
- downloaded annual report from the corporate web site.
- downloaded Form 10-K data from the SEC's EDGAR database on the internet.

Your instructor will provide data for you or indicate which is format is required for your particular class. If your instructor allows you to choose your own corporation, choose one that interests you. For example, if you enjoy the latest fashion, you may want to select a corporation that manufactures or sells apparel. You may want to select the corporation that produces a soft drink you enjoy. Or, you may want to select a corporation located in your community or state. More specific information on how to obtain annual financial data is in Appendix A.

You may also want to consider requesting the annual reports of corporations that compete with the corporation you select. Receiving more than one annual report will only increase your exposure to the financial statements!

When you receive the annual report, familiarize yourself with the contents by reviewing it carefully. Annual reports usually have a contents page to help you locate specific items. After completing your review, read the instructions and begin the project.

Completion time ranges from eight to twenty hours. The average completion time is approximately ten hours.

INSTRUCTIONS

In this project, you should answer questions about the operating results and financial position of a corporation. Answers to all questions will be obtained directly from the corporation's annual report.

Locating Information in the Annual Report

Some reports will not contain information requested in the project. In other words, some annual reports will not "fit the mold." If this is the case, seek the help of your instructor to determine if you understand the annual report correctly. When the structure of the financial statements make it impossible to answer certain questions, simply indicate why you are unable to answer the question in the project.

The annual financial data for publicly-traded corporations appear in the EDGAR database on the SEC website. Most corporations also disclose their annual financial data on their corporate web site. Once in these sites, you may use the Find command in your internet browser to locate the information you need. Key words to assist you in this type of search are provided throughout this document where a mouse icon appears (⌐⊕).

Chronological Terms

In this project, the term "current" refers to the year for which the annual report was prepared. For corporations with December 31 year-ends, annual reports are usually issued in February or March of the following year.

Using Excel Spreadsheets for Financial Analysis

An Excel spreadsheet to accompany this project is available on the internet at www.mhhe.com/pasewark5e. The spreadsheet may be used to confirm many of the calculations you make in the project. Instructions on how to use the spreadsheet are in Appendix C. Portions of the project that may be enhanced by using the Excel spreadsheet are indicated by the file icon (⊞).

Additional Help

If you need to review terms or accounting principles discussed in the annual report. Refer to the textbook used in your class for details.

GETTING ACQUAINTED WITH THE ANNUAL REPORT

GENERAL INFORMATION

General information may be in several places of annual reports. This information generally appears at the beginning of the report, the end of the annual report, or on or near the inside back cover.

Answer the following questions about the annual report you have selected:

1. What is the name of the corporation you will analyze?

    _____

2. The corporate headquarters is located in what city?

    _____

3. When is the fiscal year end of the corporation?

    _____20_____

4. What is (are) the primary product(s) or service(s) of the corporation?

    _____   _____

    _____   _____

    _____   _____

5. A transfer agent facilitates the issuance of capital stock and the payment of cash dividends. Who is the corporation's transfer agent and where is the agent located?

    Transfer Agent   _____

    City where transfer
    agent is located   _____

6. The corporation must show high and low selling prices of the corporation's common stock each quarter for the last two years. Chart the common stock prices over the last two years (🖫 Seasonality worksheet):

   a. In the chart, mark the high price of each quarter with an **X**. Then, mark the low price of each quarter with a ●.
   b. Connect the high prices with a line to indicate the trend. Then connect the low prices with a dotted line.

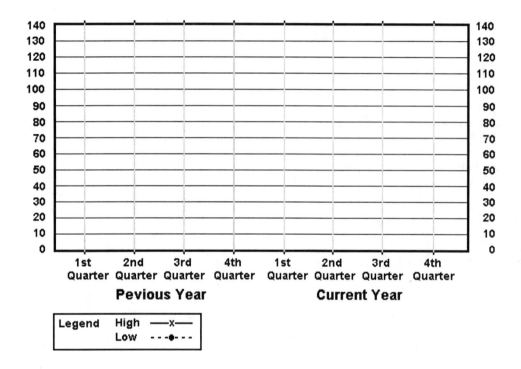

7. Describe the trend in the price of the common stock over the last two years (for example, was it upward, downward, volatile, or constant).

_____

_____

8. Did the stock trade within a narrow or wide range?

_____

_____

INTERNET INFORMATION

The Corporate Website

1. What is the internet address for the corporation?

    Internet Address   _____

2. The following items normally appear in annual reports sent to the stockholders. Check each of the items that appear in the web site:

___ Operating Highlights	___ Notes to the Financial Statements
___ Management Discussion and Analysis	___ Multi-Year Financial Summary
___ The Primary Financial Statements	___ Report of the Independent Auditors

3. What are other purposes of this web site?

___ Describe the corporation	___ Publicize corporate citizenship
___ Publicize recent corporate events	___ Provide customer service information
___ Advertise corporate products	___ Provide product financing information
___ Identify the location of retail sales sites	___ Provide employment information

The Securities and Exchange Commission's EDGAR Database

The primary purpose of the Securities and Exchange Commission (SEC) is to protect investors and maintain the integrity of the securities markets. The commission regulates the issuance and trading of publicly-held securities.

The SEC requires filing of several forms including annual financial reports (10-K), quarterly financial reports (10-Q), registration statements for newly-offered securities (S-1, S-3), current reports of material events or changes (8-K), and others. These forms are publicly available on the internet (www.sec.gov) in a database called the Electronic Data Gathering, Analysis, and Retrieval system (EDGAR). A tutorial on how to use EDGAR is at www.sec.gov/edgar/quickedgar.htm.

Form 10-K is particularly useful in analyzing a corporation because it contains information that sometimes does not appear in the annual report to stockholders. For example Form 10-K contains a detailed description of the business (Item 1) and its properties (Item 2), a description of executive compensation (Item 11), and description of management controls (Item 14).

Find the latest Form 10-K of your corporation and answer the following questions:

1. What is the date of the latest Form 10-K? _____

2. What is the primary Standardized Industrial Code?(🖰 standardized industrial) _____

3. The Central Index Key (CIK) is a unique number assigned to corporations that file with the SEC.

    What is the corporation's CIK? (🖰 central index) _____

THE PRIMARY FINANCIAL STATEMENTS

INCOME STATEMENT

The income statement (sometimes called the "statement of earnings" or statement of operations") is usually the first major financial statement appearing in the report. The income statement summarizes corporate revenues and expenses for a period of time. Corporations provide three years of income statements for comparative purposes (provided the corporation has been in operation for three years).

Growth in Revenues and Profits

1. Revenue growth is determined by the percentage increase (decrease) of revenues in comparison with the previous year:

$$\frac{\text{Current Year Revenue - Previous Year Revenue}}{\text{Previous Year Revenue}}$$

Indicate the growth in revenue during the current year (⊞ Ratio Analysis worksheet):

_____ - _____ = _____ %

2. Corporations are required to show summarized historical data. Label the vertical axis of the following chart with a scale that will accommodate revenue over the last five years. Then chart the level of revenue for the last five years (⊞ Trend Analysis worksheet).

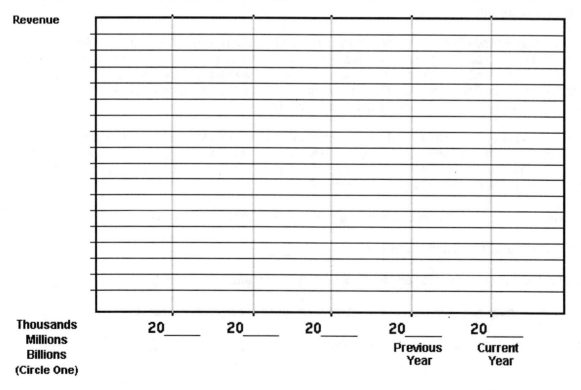

Revenue

| 20____ | 20____ | 20____ | 20____ Previous Year | 20____ Current Year |

Thousands
Millions
Billions
(Circle One)

6

3. Did revenue increase or decrease over the last few years? An explanation of the change in revenue is often contained in the management discussion and analysis section. What reasons did management give for the change?

_____

_____

_____

_____

_____

_____

_____

_____

_____

4. Trends in corporate profits are determined by calculating the percentage of increase (decrease) in income from continuing operations over the previous year. Income from continuing operations is net income without the effects of any discontinued operations, extraordinary items, or cumulative effects of accounting changes.

<u>Current Year Income from Continuing Operations - Previous Year Income from Continuing Operations</u>
Previous Year Income from Continuing Operations

Determine the growth in profits during the current year (⊟ Ratio Analysis worksheet):

$$\frac{\rule{4cm}{0.4pt} - \rule{4cm}{0.4pt}}{\rule{9cm}{0.4pt}} = \rule{2cm}{0.4pt} \%$$

Common-Size Analysis

Common-size (or percentage) analysis expresses items in a financial statement as a percentage of a single item. This analysis permits comparisons between two or more years, or between two or more corporations. For an income statement, certain items are usually expressed as a percentage of revenue. Perform common-size analysis in relation to revenue for the following items in the income statement for the current and previous years (🖫 Ratio Analysis worksheet):

	Current Year	Previous Year
Revenue	100.0%	100.0%
Cost of Goods / Services	_____	_____
Gross Profit	_____	_____
Operating Expense	_____	_____
Interest Expense	_____	_____
Research and Development Expense	_____	_____
Income Tax Expense	_____	_____
Income from Continuing Operations	_____	_____
Net Income	_____	_____

Based on your common-size analysis, compare current year operating results in terms of cost control, debt servicing, tax burdens, and profitability. Information concerning the reasons for change may be found in the management discussion and analysis.

1. **Product or Service Cost Control** - Did the percent of product costs (cost of goods or services) to revenue change in the current year in comparison to the previous year? What are possible explanations for changes, if any, that may have occurred?

_____

_____

_____

_____

2. **Operating Cost Control** - Did the percentage of operating costs (selling and administrative expenses) to revenue change in the current year in comparison to the previous year? What are possible explanations for changes, if any, that may have occurred?

_____

_____

_____

3. **Debt Servicing** - How did the percentage of interest expense to revenue compare to the previous year? What are possible explanations for changes, if any?

_____

_____

_____

4. **Tax Burden** - Did the tax expense as a percentage of total revenue change in the current year? What are possible explanations for these changes, if any? (Without knowledge of the tax laws applying to the corporation, it may be impossible to determine specific reasons for the change.)

_____

_____

_____

5. **Profitability** - How did net income as a percentage of revenue change in the current year? What items in the income statement explain the change in income from continuing operations as a percentage of revenue?

_____

_____

_____

6. **Other Income Statement Items** - Generally accepted accounting principles require amounts related to discontinued operations, extraordinary items, and cumulative effects of accounting changes be shown, net of taxes, at the bottom of the income statement. If any of these items are present, describe the nature and amount.

_____

_____

BALANCE SHEET

The balance sheet summarizes assets and equities (liabilities and stockholders' equity) of a corporation. Assets are usually grouped in one of five categories: current assets, investments, fixed assets (sometimes referred to as property, plant, and equipment), intangible assets, and other assets. Liabilities are typically grouped into current liabilities and long-term liabilities.

Asset Growth

The "size" of a corporation is commonly measured by the amount of total assets on the corporation's balance sheet. A corporation is considered "growing" if total assets increase from one year to the next. The rate of growth is measured by the change in total assets divided by the total assets of the previous year:

$$\frac{\text{Current Year Total Assets - Previous Year Total Assets}}{\text{Previous Year Total Assets}}$$

1. Determine the percentage of growth in assets (🖫 Ratio Analysis worksheet):

    _____ - _____ = _____ %

2. Did total assets increase or decrease? What were the primary reasons for the change in total assets?

    _____

    _____

    _____

    _____

    _____

    _____

    _____

Common-Size Analysis

In the balance sheet, common-size analysis is performed by expressing accounts as a percentage of total assets. These percentages are often compared to the percentage of previous years or to the percentages calculated for another corporation in the same industry. Complete the common-size analysis for the following items in the balance sheet (⊟ Ratio Analysis worksheet):

	Current Year	Previous Year
Current Assets	_____	_____
Long-term Investments	_____	_____
Fixed Assets	_____	_____
Intangibles	_____	_____
Other Assets	_____	_____
Total Assets	100%	100%
Current Liabilities	_____	_____
Total Liabilities*	_____	_____
Stockholders' Equity	_____	_____

3. Which balance sheet accounts changed the most in comparison to the previous year? What events might explain the reasons for the changes in these accounts?

_____

_____

_____

_____

_____

_____

CASH FLOW STATEMENT

The purpose of the cash flow statement is to provide information about cash receipts, cash disbursements, and cash balances. The statement also summarizes operating, investing, and financing activities of the corporation.

1. Indicate the cash flows resulting from operating, investing, and financing activities. Be sure to identify whether the cash flow was positive or negative. Then indicate the change in cash, and the beginning and ending cash balances:

Cash Flow Activity	Current Year	Previous Year
Operating	_____	_____
Investing	_____	_____
Financing	_____	_____
Increase (decrease) in cash	_____	_____
Beginning cash balance	_____	_____
Ending cash balance	_____	_____

2. What were the three most significant sources of cash?

_____

_____

_____

3. What were the three most significant uses of cash?

_____

_____

_____

4. Chart the net income and cash flow from operations over the last three years (🖫 Trend Analysis worksheet):

   a. Label the vertical axis of the following chart with a scale that will accommodate net income and cash flow from operations over the last three years.

   b. Mark the level of net income for each year with an **X**. Then, mark the cash flow from operations for each year with a ●

   c. Connect the net income amounts with a line to indicate the trend. Then connect the amounts of cash flow from operations with a dotted line.

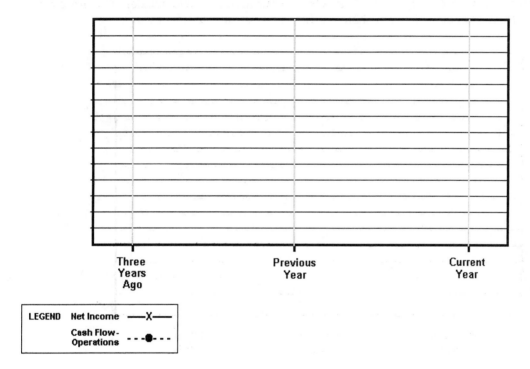

5. Based on a comparison of the income statement to the statement of cash flows, what caused the greatest differences between net income (loss) and cash flow from operations?

_____

_____

_____

STATEMENT OF CHANGES IN STOCKHOLDERS' EQUITY

The statement of changes in stockholders' equity explains the changes in individual equity balances during the year. If the retained earnings are the only capital account that changed during the fiscal year, a statement of changes in retained earnings is often presented instead.

Most annual reports show the statement of changes in stockholders' equity as a formal financial statement following the balance sheet and income statement; however, some corporations show the statement of stockholders' equity in the notes of the financial statements.

Shares Outstanding

Label the vertical axis of the following chart with a scale that will accommodate number of shares over the last three years. Then chart the number of shares outstanding over the last three years.

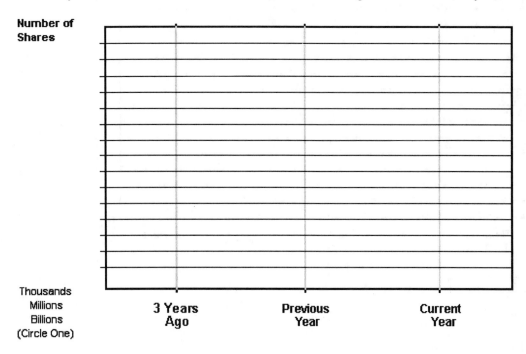

Did the number of shares increase, decrease, or remain constant? What were the reasons, if any, for the changes?

_____

_____

_____

_____

14

Retained Earnings

Record the amounts in the statement of changes in stockholders' equity for the following items:

	<u>Current Year</u>	<u>Previous Year</u>
Beginning Retained Earnings	$_____	$_____
Dividends (if any)	_____	_____
Net Income (Net Loss)	_____	_____
Other Items	_____	_____
Ending Retained Earnings	$_____	$_____

Comprehensive Income

Comprehensive income represents the change in equity (net assets) of a corporation during the year from transactions other than those resulting from investments and distributions to owners. Comprehensive income usually differs from net income as a result of:

- Changes in the value of certain investments and financial instruments
- Amounts associated with the recognition of a minimum liability of a pension plan
- Certain translation adjustments for foreign currency
- Certain transactions with derivative securities

Record the items that explain the difference between net income and comprehensive income in the current year. If the corporation does not have any items that make comprehensive income different from net income, enter the same amount for net income and comprehensive income.

Net Income (loss) $ _____

Items explaining the difference in
net income and comprehensive income:

_____ $ _____

_____ $ _____

_____ $ _____

_____ $ _____

Comprehensive income (loss) $ _____

NOTES AND SUPPORTING SCHEDULES TO THE FINANCIAL STATEMENTS

The notes and supporting schedules to the financial statements are located after the financial statements in the annual report. Notes, sometimes called "footnotes," provide additional explanations, descriptions, and supporting information not conveniently displayed within the body of the financial statements. Supporting schedules are tables that provide more detailed information about certain items in the primary financial statements.

Inexperienced financial statement users sometimes regard the notes and supporting schedules as unimportant. However, most of the information contained in the notes and schedules are required by GAAP and can make a difference in a decision the financial statement users make concerning the corporation. For example, a contingent liability considered "reasonably possible" may be shown in the notes rather than the liability section of the balance sheet. A financial statement user who ignores the notes would not be aware of contingencies that may affect the corporation in the future.

The first note in an annual report usually summarizes the significant accounting policies used by the corporation when preparing the financial statements. This note is generally followed by notes addressing more specific topics.

It is possible that some of the following topics may not apply to the corporation you selected. For example, if the company does not have a pension plan, there is no need for a pension note. If a note is not applicable, write "NA" in the blank. Examine the notes carefully before deciding the topic does not apply. Answer the following questions concerning the notes to the financial statements.

Cash and Cash Equivalents Corporations often report "cash equivalents" along with cash on the balance sheet (SFAS 95). Cash equivalents usually include short-maturity deposits and liquid savings accounts. How does the corporation define their cash equivalents? (🖰 cash equivalents, cash, liquid)

_____

_____

Accounts Receivable Corporations with receivables must disclose the net amount due and any allowance for amounts deemed uncollectible. The percentage of uncollectibles is calculated by dividing the allowance for uncollectibles by the gross accounts receivable. Gross accounts receivable are net receivables before the allowance for uncollectibles is removed.

$$\text{Percent Uncollectible} = \frac{\text{Allowance for Uncollectibles}}{\text{Gross Accounts Receivable}}$$

Determine the percentage of uncollectibles for the current and previous year (🖥 Ratio Analysis worksheet):

Current Year	Previous Year

_____ = _____ %   _____ = _____ %

The receivables turnover ratio is an indication of the number of times a year the corporation collects its accounts receivables. The ratio is determined by dividing credit sales by the average accounts receivable. Average accounts receivable is usually determined by dividing beginning and ending accounts receivable by two.

$$\text{Receivable Turnover} = \frac{\text{Credit Sales}}{\text{Average Receivables}}$$

Compute the receivables turnover ratio for the corporation in the current and previous year. If credit sales are not available, assume that all sales are on credit. Beginning accounts receivable for the previous year may be unavailable in the current annual report. The amount may be obtained from a previous year annual report (for example, Form 10-K on EDGAR at www.sec.gov) (🖫 Ratio Analysis worksheet).

<u>Current Year</u>   <u>Previous Year</u>

_____ = times   _____ = times

How did the receivable turnover ratio change from the previous year to the current year? What are the implications of this change? (🖑 accounts receivable, uncollectible, bad debt)

_____

_____

_____

Inventories Material classifications of inventories must be itemized on the balance sheet or in a corresponding note (ARB 43, Chapter 4, Paragraph 15). Is the inventory classified into more than one category? If so, what are those categories?

_____   _____

_____   _____

_____   _____

The inventory flow method [for example, first-in, first-out (FIFO); average; or last-in, first-out (LIFO)] selected by a corporation can significantly affect the amount allocated to inventory on the balance sheet and cost of goods sold on the income statement.

A corporation is required to disclose flow method(s) used to value its inventory (ARB 43, Chapter 3A, Paragraph 9). In some cases, the corporation will value foreign and domestic inventory groups in different ways. What method(s) is (are) used to account for inventories? (✓ inventory, last-in, first-in, first-out)

Inventory Group   Inventory Flow Method

Domestic Inventories   _____

Foreign Inventories   _____

If the corporation uses a LIFO flow method, it must disclose the LIFO reserve, which is the difference between the LIFO inventory amount and the current value or FIFO inventory amount typically used for internal reporting. If the corporation uses LIFO to value the inventory, indicate the following for the current year:

Inventory using LIFO (as shown on the balance sheet) $ _____

LIFO Reserve $ _____

Inventory at Current Cost / FIFO / Replacement Cost $ _____

The inventory turnover ratio is an indication of the number of times a year the corporation sells its inventory during a year. It is determined by dividing cost of sales by the average inventory. Average inventory is determined by dividing the sum of beginning and ending inventory by two.

$$\text{Inventory Turnover} = \frac{\text{Cost of Sales}}{\text{Average Inventory}}$$

Compute the inventory turnover ratio for the corporation in the current and previous year. If beginning inventory for the previous year is not available in the current annual report it may be obtained from a previous year annual report (for example, Form 10-K on EDGAR at www.sec.gov) (▣ Ratio Analysis worksheet).

Current Year   Previous Year

_____ = times   _____ = times

How did the inventory turnover ratio change from the previous year to the current year? What are the implications of this change?

_____

_____

Investments Investments are classified as trading securities (intended to generate near-term profits), held-to-maturity (debt investments that will be held for the investment life), securities available for sale (SFAS 115) or equity investments (APB 18). Does the corporation hold investments? If so, indicate the value of these investments in each of the following categories for the current year. (☞ trading securities, held-to-maturity, available for sale, equity investment)

Investment Category	Current Investments	Long-Term Investments
Trading Securities	$ _____	
Held-to-Maturity Securities	$ _____	$ _____
Securities Available for Sale	$ _____	$ _____
Equity Investments		$ _____

Property and Depreciation If material, separate categories of property, plant, and equipment should be disclosed. Identify the categories of property, plant, and equipment. (☞ buildings, machinery, equipment, land)

_____   _____

_____   _____

_____   _____

Corporations must disclose the depreciation method(s) used to value property, plant, and equipment (APB 12). In some cases, the corporations will use more than one depreciation method. What methods(s) is (are) used to depreciate property, plant, and equipment? (☞ depreciation, straight-line, accelerated)

Fixed Asset Group	Depreciation Method
_____	_____
_____	_____
_____	_____
_____	_____
_____	_____

Impairment of fixed assets occurs when the market value of an asset is significantly lower than the carrying amount and that amount is not considered recoverable. Losses resulting from impairment of long-lived assets must be charged against income (SFAS 121 and 144). Were any assets recognized as impaired during the current year? If so, what was the nature of the impaired assets and the amount charged against income to recognize the impairment? (🖰 impairment, 121, 144)

_____

_____

_____

An approximation of the remaining usefulness of property, plant, and equipment may be determined by computing the percentage that assets are depreciated. The ratio is calculated by dividing accumulated depreciation by the gross depreciable fixed assets. Depreciable fixed assets do not include land or construction in progress.

$$\text{Percentage of Fixed Asset Depreciation} = \frac{\text{Accumulated Depreciation}}{\text{Gross Depreciable Fixed Assets}}$$

Calculate the percentage of fixed asset depreciation for the company in the current and previous year.

<u>Current Year</u>   <u>Previous Year</u>

_____ =   %   _____ =   %

How did the percentage of fixed asset depreciation change from previous year to the current year? What might be the reasons for this change? What are the implications of this change for the future?

_____

_____

_____

_____

The fixed asset turnover ratio indicates how efficiently fixed assets are used to generate revenue. The ratio is particularly useful in a capital intensive corporation in which plant and equipment are used to generate revenue. The ratio is calculated by dividing revenue by the fixed assets held during the year.

$$\text{Fixed Asset Turnover Ratio} = \frac{\text{Revenue}}{\text{Average Fixed Assets}}$$

Compute the fixed asset turnover ratio for the corporation in the current and previous year. If beginning fixed assets for the previous year is not available in the current annual report, it may be obtained by from a previous year annual report (for example, Form 10-K on EDGAR at www.sec.gov) (⌨ Ratio Analysis worksheet).

<u>Current Year</u>   <u>Previous Year</u>

_____ = times   _____ = times

Capitalized Leases Some corporations lease, rather than purchase, property, or equipment. Capitalized leases transfer the benefits and risks of ownership to the lessee. An asset and a liability approximately equal to the present value of the rental payments is recorded. The asset associated with a capital lease is periodically amortized in the same way that owned assets are depreciated. In addition, the lessee will make rental payment that consists of interest and principal. If the corporation uses capital leases (⌐ lease, capital(ized)) lease, lease obligation, imputed interest):

What is the total amount of payments due over the life of the capitalized leases?

$ _____

Of the total payments due for capitalized leases, what amount is considered to be imputed interest?

$ _____

What is the long-term liability associated with leases recognized on the balance sheet?

$ _____

Assuming the corporation does not enter into additional lease agreements, what will be the amount of the payment associated with capital leases next year?

$ _____

Operating Leases Operating leases are legal obligations that require the corporation to make periodic payments for several years. These leases do not require recording of a long-term asset or liability. However, GAAP requires disclosure of the expected payments over the life of the lease. (🖰 lease, operating lease) What was the total obligation associated with operating leases?

$ _____

What was the rent expense associated with the operating leases in the current year?

$ _____

Assuming the corporation does not enter into additional lease agreements, what will be the payment for operating leases next year?

$ _____

Long-term Debt Long-term debt is usually organized by type of lender (for example, loans from banks and bond issues are usually grouped separately). Corporations disclose interest rates, due dates, collateral, and loan covenants of long-term debt. What long-term debt obligations does the corporation have? If the corporation has more than five debt instruments, list the five largest. (🖰 debt, credit facility, loan, maturity)

Instrument	Rate	Amount
_____	_____ %	$ _____
_____	_____ %	$ _____
_____	_____ %	$ _____
_____	_____ %	$ _____
_____	_____ %	$ _____

Debt payments for each of the next five years must be disclosed. In which of the next five years is the most long-term debt due?

Year _____   Amount to be paid $ _____

Pension Plans A pension plan is usually the most significant of all post-retirement benefits. In general, these plans are classified as:

- **Defined Contribution Plans** (for example, 401(k) plans) – The employer makes periodic payments to employees to be placed into designated retirement account. No promise is made concerning the amount available at the time of retirement.
- **Defined Benefit Plans** – The employer promises a specified amount (usually based on ending salaries and years of service) to retired employees.

Both defined benefit and defined contribution plans have associated expenses. If the corporation has either of these types of plans, what was the pension expense (benefit) associated with the plan(s) for the current year? (🖑 pension, benefits, retirement, defined contribution, defined benefit)

Defined Contribution Pension Expense $ _____

Defined Benefit Pension Expense (Benefit) $ _____

Corporations with defined benefit plans are required to disclose an estimate of the cumulative obligation owed by the pension plan. The benefit obligation is the present value of the benefits owed to current employees based on their expected future salaries. How much is the benefit obligation at the end of the current year?

      $ _____

Corporations with defined benefit plans must also disclose the market value of the assets currently held in the pension fund. What was the fair value of the retirement plan assets at the end of the current year?

      $ _____

Based on a comparison of the obligation and the assets of the plan(s), would you say the plan(s) is (are) adequately funded? Why or why not?

_____

_____

What was the prepaid pension cost or accrued pension liability included in the balance sheet of the corporation?

                                    Circle One:
      $ _____   Prepaid Pension Asset
                                    Accrued Pension Liability

What was the cash amount contributed to the defined benefit pension plan during the current year?

      $ _____

What was the amount of defined benefit pension benefits paid to retirees during the current year?

$ _____

Post-Retirement Benefits Other Than Pensions Post-retirement benefits are programs providing cash and services to former employees. In addition to pension plans, these programs may include health care, dental care, life insurance, and savings plans. The accounting for post-retirement benefits is similar to that of the pension plan (SFAS 106). (⌐ benefits, post-retirement, non-pension)

What was the expense (benefit) associated with non-pension post-retirement benefits?

$ _____

What was the benefit obligation for the non-pension post-retirement benefit plan(s)?

$ _____

What was the fair market value of the assets held for non-pension post-retirement benefit plans?

$ _____

Based on a comparison of the obligation and the assets of the post-retirement benefit plan(s), would you say the plan(s) are adequately funded? Why or why not?

_____

_____

What was the non-pension post-retirement benefit liability (asset) included on the balance sheet?

$ _____

Circle One:
Prepaid Post-Retirement Benefit Asset
Accrued Post-Retirement Benefit Liability

What was the cash amount contributed to non-pension post-retirement benefit plans during the current year?

$ _____

What was the amount of non-pension post-retirement benefits paid to retirees during the current year?

$ _____

Income Taxes Income tax expense is often one of the largest expense categories on the income statement. Income tax expense is determined by applying a tax rate to the portion of income taxed. However, the federal government will often allow payment of taxes to be deferred to later years. Deferred taxes result from differences between the way net income and taxable income are determined. GAAP requires corporations to disclose (either in a note or on the financial statement) the current tax expense and the amount of taxes deferred to a later year (SFAS 109). (⇗ income tax, tax(es), deferred tax, 109)

What was the income tax expense (or provision) for the current year appearing in the income statement?

$ _____

According to the note for income taxes, what portion of the current year's income tax expense (federal, state, and international) has been deferred to future periods?

$ _____

What was the effective tax rate for corporation for the current year? (⇗ effective tax rate, statutory)

_____%

Deferred tax assets and liabilities result from differences between corporate accounting and the determination of taxable income. What amount is disclosed in the notes as:

Deferred tax asset $ _____

Deferred tax liability $ _____

		Circle One:
Net deferred tax amount	$ _____	Asset
		Liability

What significant activities resulted in recognition of deferred tax liabilities that are not yet due to a tax authority?

_____

_____

What significant activities led to the recognition of deferred tax assets that will be utilized in the future?

_____

_____

Stock-Based Compensation Options are an opportunity to purchase shares of stock at a guaranteed price for a specified period of time. They are often issued to employees as an incentive to perform in a manner that increases the value of the corporation (and, thus, increases the market price of the stock). However, these options potentially dilute the ownership interest of existing stockholders. GAAP requires a disclosure of these securities and their financial effects (SFAS 123). (☞ incentive, options, stock-based, compensation, 123)

Options are considered *outstanding* if they are granted by the corporation, but not yet exercised, cancelled, or expired. Options are *exercisable* when they are held for an appropriate period and are currently eligible for purchasing stock. At the end of the current year:

Options to purchase _____ shares were outstanding

at an average exercise price of $ _____per share.

Options to purchase _____ shares were exercisable

at an average exercise price of $ _____per share.

During the current year:

_____ shares were purchased by exercising options.

_____ shares were no longer available for exercise because the options expired or canceled.

Corporations may elect to recognize an employee compensation expense based on the fair value of options issued during the year. If they do not recognize this expense, they must disclose a pro forma income amount that recognizes the decrease in net income that would have occurred had an employee compensation expense been recognized. In the blank below, indicate either (1) the expense associated with the issuance of the options for the current year, or (2) the difference in pro forma and reported net income that represents the value of the options granted during the year:

$ _____

Circle One:
Stock-Based Compensation Expense
Difference in Pro-Forma and Reported Net Income

How many shares does the corporation have available for grant (sometimes referred to as "on hand" or in treasury)?

_____ shares

Are there enough shares to accommodate exercisable options?   Yes   No   (circle one)

Are there enough shares to accommodate outstanding options?   Yes   No   (circle one)

Segmental and Geographic Information GAAP (SFAS 131) requires identification of key information concerning operating segments. In addition, if the corporation operates in several geographic areas, information concerning the financial results of major geographic area should also be reported. If the corporation discloses disaggregated information, indicate the primary business and/or geographic segments (✐ segment, geographic, 131):

Operating Segments   Geographic Areas

_____   _____

_____   _____

_____   _____

_____   _____

_____   _____

Contingencies Contingent liabilities are financial obligations that depend on the occurrence (or nonoccurrence) of future events. Disclosure of these obligations depends on whether or not the future event is probable, reasonably possible, or remote (SFAS 5). For example, if losing a $2,000,000 lawsuit is probable, the amount is shown as a liability and an expense and the lawsuit is described in a note. If the loss of the lawsuit is reasonably possible, no liability is recognized; however, the lawsuit is described in a note. Remote losses need not be disclosed.

Identify any contingencies that potentially affect the financial position of the corporation. Are these contingencies probable or reasonably possible? Were any of the contingencies reported as an expense on the income statement and a liability on the balance sheet? (✐ contingency(ies), legal, lawsuit)

_____

_____

_____

_____

_____

_____

_____

Interim (Quarterly) Financial Data Disclosure of quarterly data aids the financial statement user in determining the seasonality of corporate operations. For example, American manufacturers of confectionery will typically experience much higher sales in the quarter that includes the Halloween and Christmas holidays. Large public companies are required by the SEC (Item 302(a), Reg. S-K) to include quarterly amounts for revenues, gross profit, net income, and net income per share. (🖰 interim, quarterly) (💾 Seasonality worksheet)

Chart the quarterly revenue for the corporation over the current year:

a. Label the vertical axis of the following chart with a scale that will accommodate the quarterly revenue that occurred throughout the current year.

b. Mark the level of revenue for each year with an **X**.

c. Connect the revenue amounts with a line to indicate the trend.

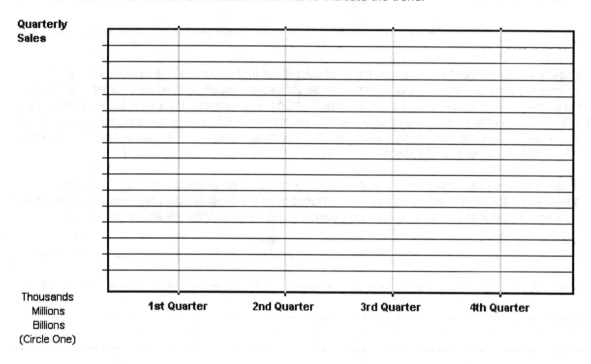

Do you detect significant fluctuations in quarterly data for the corporation? If so, explain the reasons for the fluctuation(s)?

_____

_____

_____

_____

REPORT OF THE INDEPENDENT ACCOUNTANTS

Auditing is a process by which an independent accounting firm accumulates and evaluates data to determine whether the financial statements are presented in accordance with GAAP. The Securities and Exchange Commission requires an annual audit for all companies whose capital stock is traded on a recognized stock exchange.

The purpose of the audit report is to communicate the findings of the auditor to financial statement users. The auditor's report usually appears immediately after the notes to the financial statements. Who is the corporation's auditor and where is the auditor located?

Auditor   _____

City where auditor
is located   _____

An audit report usually consists of three parts that (1) define the responsibility of management, (2) describe the nature of the audit, and (3) express an opinion on whether the financial statements are fairly presented and in conformity with generally accepted accounting principles. The following are types of audit opinions that commonly in annual reports:

An *unqualified opinion* states that, in the auditor's opinion, the financial statements are in conformity with generally accepted accounting principles and that the auditor is reasonably assured that the financial statements are free from material misstatement.

A *qualified opinion* is issued when the auditor detects non-pervasive departures from GAAP or non-pervasive scope limitations. A qualified opinion includes the words "except for" in the paragraph in which the auditor expresses an opinion.

Disclaimer of opinion occurs when the auditor experiences severe limitations on the scope of the audit or if a nonindependent relationship exists between the auditor and the client. Each of these conditions makes it impossible for the auditor to express an opinion on the financial statements. A disclaimer of opinion will clearly state that the auditor does not render an opinion.

An *adverse opinion* is given only when the auditor believes the financial statements are materially misstated or misleading. An adverse opinion will state specifically that the financial statements do not in conform to GAAP.

Read the auditor's opinion carefully, then answer the following questions concerning the content of the opinion.

1.   Place an X by the type of opinion expressed by the auditor:

☐   Unqualified   ☐   Disclaimer of opinion

☐   Qualified   ☐   Adverse opinion

2. An auditor's report will state the responsibility of the auditor. What is the responsibility of the auditor with regard to the financial statements?

_____

_____

_____

_____

_____

3. What guidelines does the auditor use to conduct the audit?

_____

_____

_____

4. Does the auditor believe the financial statements were presented fairly? What statements in the audit opinion support your conclusion?

_____

_____

_____

_____

_____

RATIO ANALYSIS

Ratio analysis is a way to compare current performance and financial position to (1) previous years, and (2) other corporations. Calculate the following ratios for your corporation. You should show all of your calculations. In other words, indicate the components of the numerator and the denominator for each ratio. (⊞ The Ratio Analysis worksheet will be useful throughout this section.)

ANALYSIS OF PROFITABILITY

Ratios of profitability indicate the degree of success of the corporation's operations during the year. Profitability ratios show the amount of resources required to generate profits and the availability of profits to stockholders. These ratios are often used as a means for stockholders to evaluate the performance of corporate management.

1. Profit Margin

The profit margin on revenue shows the relation of profits to revenue. The percentage is computed by dividing income from continuing operations by net revenue for the year. Income from continuing operations is net income without the effects of any discontinued operations, extraordinary items, or cumulative effects of accounting changes.

$$\frac{\text{Profit}}{\text{Margin}} = \frac{\text{Income from Continuing Operations}}{\text{Net Revenue}}$$

A higher profit margin indicates less revenue is needed to generate a desired level of profit. Compute the profit margin on sales for the current and previous years:

Current Year   Previous Year

_____ = _____ %   _____ = _____ %

2. Return on Assets

The return on assets (ROA) ratio indicates how well the assets of the corporation are utilized to achieve a profit. The ratio demonstrates potential earning similar to the way a savings account interest rate indicates how much you can earn on money invested in savings. The percentage is computed by dividing income from continuing operations by average total assets held over the year. Average assets are usually computed by adding current year total assets to previous year total assets and dividing by two.

$$\frac{\text{Return}}{\text{on Assets}} = \frac{\text{Income from Continuing Operations for Current Year}}{(\text{Current Year Total Assets} + \text{Previous Year Total Assets}) / 2}$$

Total assets for the current and previous years appear on the balance sheet; however, because a balance sheet typically shows only two years of data, previous year total assets may appear in another section of the of the annual report. Corporations differ on where they show data concerning previous years. (You may have to examine the annual report closely to find historical data.) Compute the return on assets for the current and previous year:

<u>Current Year</u>   <u>Previous Year</u>

_____ = _____ %   _____ = _____ %

3. Return on Stockholders' Equity

Return on stockholders' equity is similar to return on assets except it removes the effect of funds the corporation has borrowed. It is calculated by dividing income from continuing operations by the average stockholders' equity through the year.

$$\text{Return on Equity} = \frac{\text{Income from Continuing Operations for the Current Year}}{(\text{Current Year Equity} + \text{Previous Year Equity}) / 2}$$

Total equity for the current and previous years appears on the balance sheet; however, because a balance sheet typically shows only two years of data, previous year total equity may appear in another section of the annual report. Compute the return on stockholders' equity for the current and previous year:

<u>Current Year</u>   <u>Previous Year</u>

_____ = _____ %   _____ = _____ %

What corporate characteristic causes the return on assets and return on equity percentages to be different?

_____

_____

_____

_____

_____

All three of the preceding ratios indicate profitability by comparing income from continuing operations to another number in the income statement or balance sheet. In comparison to the previous year, has the corporation improved its ability to generate a profit? Justify your answer based on the ratios you calculated.

_____

_____

_____

_____

_____

4. Earnings Per Share

The earnings per share ratio (EPS) represents the amount of earnings attributable to each share of stock in the corporation. The ratio is considered so important that GAAP requires EPS disclosure on the face of the income statement. In its simplest form, EPS is calculated by dividing net income, less preferred stock dividends, by the average number of common shares outstanding. If the corporation has income or losses from discontinued operations, extraordinary items, or cumulative effects of accounting changes, the effects of these items on earning per share must be disclosed separately.

In the spaces below, record the basic earnings per share for continuing operations as it appears on the income statement:

Current Year	Previous Year
Dollars	Dollars
_____ Per Share	_____ Per Share

Was the amount for the current year better or worse than the ratio of the previous year? Was the change in EPS a result of changes in the numerator or the denominator of the ratio? Explain.

_____

_____

_____

_____

The equity section of a balance sheet may have dilutive securities (such as options, convertible bonds and convertible preferred stock) that can decrease EPS by increasing the number of shares in the denominator. In this case, the corporation may be required to show a diluted EPS in addition to the basic EPS. Were diluted EPS disclosed by the corporation? If so, what equity securities in the balance sheet have the potential of increasing the EPS denominator?

_____

_____

_____

_____

5. Cash Dividends per Share

Cash dividends per share is similar to earnings per share except the numerator excludes the portion of earnings retained in the corporation. In other words, the ratio indicates the amount of cash dividends the stockholder received during the year for each share of stock owned.

$$\text{Cash Dividends Per Share} = \frac{\text{Cash Dividends Paid to Common Stockholders}}{(\text{Current Year Number of Shares} + \text{Last Year Number of Shares}) / 2}$$

The dividend paid to common stockholders appears on the statement of retained earnings. The number of common stock shares outstanding appears on the balance sheet; however, because a balance sheet typically shows only two years of data, the previous year number of shares may appear in the selected financial data section of the annual report. Compute the cash dividends per share for the current and previous year:

Current Year		Previous Year	
_____ =	Dollars Per Share	_____ =	Dollars Per Share

6. Dividend payout ratio

The dividend payout ratio indicates the percentage of earnings returned to the stockholder rather than retained in the corporation. The ratio is computed by dividing cash dividends paid to common stockholders by the amount of income available for payment of common stock dividends.

$$\text{Dividend Payout Ratio} = \frac{\text{Cash Dividends Paid to Common Stockholders}}{\text{Net Income} - \text{Preferred Dividends Paid}}$$

The dividend paid to common and preferred stockholders appear on the statement of retained earnings. Net income appears on the income statement. Compute the dividend payout ratio for the current and previous year.

Current Year   Previous Year

_____ = _____ %   _____ = _____ %

7. Price/Earnings (P/E) Ratio

The P/E ratio measures the relationship between the earnings of the corporation and the current market price. A corporation with a P/E ratio of 15 is said to be selling at 15 times its current earnings. Some analysts believe the P/E ratio is a good measure of the future earnings power of a corporation. Companies with high P/E ratios have a stock price that reflects the expectation of higher future earnings. A lower P/E ratio may indicate that lower earnings expectations are reflected in the corporation's stock price.

$$\frac{\text{Price/Earnings}}{\text{Ratio}} = \frac{\text{Market Price Per Share}}{\text{Earnings Per Share}}$$

Calculate the P/E Ratio for the current and previous year. If end of the year market prices of common shares are not available, use an average of the high and low price during the last quarter of the year.

Current Year   Previous Year

_____ = _____ times   _____ = _____ times

In the past decade, the average P/E ratio for major corporations has ranged from 14 to 25. How does the corporation's P/E ratio compare to this average? What may be concluded concerning the expected growth of the corporation?

_____

_____

_____

_____

_____

ANALYSIS OF LIQUIDITY

A common misconception is that corporations become bankrupt because they are unprofitable. However, bankruptcy is declared because a corporation is not able to meet the current obligations to the creditors, not when the corporation lacks profitability.

Current assets are called "current" because they are converted into cash during the operating cycle. Current liabilities are liabilities liquidated by current assets or other current liabilities within the operating cycle.

Liquidity ratios indicate the corporation's ability to meet short-term cash requirements. For this reason, liquidity ratios are important to potential and existing creditors. There are two commonly computed liquidity ratios:

1. Current (or Working Capital) Ratio

The current ratio indicates whether the firm will have enough resources to meet obligations becoming due during the next period. The current ratio is the quotient of current assets divided by current liabilities. The ratio is usually expressed in a format in which the denominator is equal to "1", for example, if current assets were twice as much as current liabilities the ratio is expressed as "2:1".

$$\text{Current Ratio} = \frac{\text{Current Assets}}{\text{Current Liabilities}}$$

Strictly speaking, a ratio less than one indicates a corporation will not meet obligations due during the next period without additional resources. On the other hand, a ratio of greater than one indicates the corporation is currently is able to meet current liabilities as they become due. All components of the current ratio appear in the current sections of the balance sheet. Compute the current ratio for the current and previous year:

Current Year   Previous Year

_____ = _____ :1   _____ = _____ :1

Based on the current ratio you calculated, do you believe the corporation able to meet the current obligations as they become due? Why? Has the corporation established lines of credit with lenders to obtain working capital if needed?

_____

_____

_____

_____

Net working capital is equal to current assets minus current liabilities. What is the net working capital for the current year?

$ _____

2. Quick (or Acid-Test) Ratio

The quick ratio recognizes certain current assets are more liquid than others. For example, inventories are usually not immediately available for the liquidation of current liabilities because the corporation must first sell inventoried items to obtain cash.

The quick ratio is similar to the current ratio except the numerator includes only current assets which may be readily turned into cash. These current assets include cash, marketable securities, and net receivables.

$$\text{Quick Ratio} = \frac{\text{Cash + Marketable Securities + Net Receivables}}{\text{Current Liabilities}}$$

All components of the quick ratio appear in the current sections of the balance sheet. Compute the quick ratio for the current and previous year:

<u>Current Year</u>   <u>Previous Year</u>

_____ = :1   _____ = :1

Based on your assessment of the two liquidity ratios you calculated, did the liquidity position of the corporation strengthen or weaken compared to the previous year? What were the reasons for the change, if any?

_____

_____

_____

_____

_____

_____

_____

ANALYSIS OF SOLVENCY

Solvency ratios measure the corporation's ability to manage debt. The ratios indicate risk to long-term creditors and equity investors.

1. Debt to Total Assets

The debt to total assets ratio measures the amount of leverage used by the corporation. The ratio indicates what percentage of the assets of the corporation is financed by those other than stockholders of the corporation.

$$\frac{\text{Debt to}}{\text{Total Assets}} = \frac{\text{Total Liabilities}}{\text{Total Assets}}$$

All components of the debt to total assets ratio appear on the balance sheet. Compute the debt to total assets ratio for the current and previous year:

<u>Current Year</u>   <u>Previous Year</u>

_____ =   %   _____ =   %

How did the debt position of the corporation change over the last year? What were the sources of these changes if any?

_____

_____

_____

_____

_____

Would potential lenders prefer the debt to total assets ratio to be larger or smaller? Why?

_____

_____

_____

_____

2. Times Interest Earned Ratio

When payment of interest on debt becomes significant in proportion to the corporation's annual income, it is often evidence the corporation is spending too much of its resources servicing debt. The times interest earned ratio indicates the relationship of interest expense to income. The ratio is computed by dividing income before tax and interest expense by interest expense.

$$\text{Times Interest Earned} = \frac{\text{Net Income + Interest Expense + Tax Expense}}{\text{Interest Expense}}$$

All of the components of the times interest earned ratio appear on the income statement. Compute the times interest earned ratio for the current and previous year:

Current Year   Previous Year

_____ = _____ times   _____ = _____ times

Some believe the times interest earned ratio is more appropriately calculated on a cash basis. In this way, the ratio indicates the corporation's ability to pay interest from the cash from operations. (Cash paid in interest may differ from interest expense to the extent of accruals are made or a premium or discount is amortized.) In this case, the numerator includes cash flow from operations as it appears in the cash flow statement. The denominator is cash paid for interest, which appears in the cash flow statement or the note describing the corporation's debt obligations.

$$\text{Times Interest Earned on the Cash Basis} = \frac{\text{Cash Flow from Operations + Cash Paid for Interest}}{\text{Cash Paid for Interest}}$$

Compute the times interest earned on the cash basis for the current and previous year:

Current Year   Previous Year

_____ = _____ times   _____ = _____ times

INDUSTRY OR COMPETITOR COMPARISONS

One way to evaluate corporate success is to compare the corporation to others in the industry. Industry common-size percentages and ratios are easily obtained in most libraries. (See Appendix B, Obtaining Information for Industry Comparisons.) Most sources of industry wide data are organized by Standard Industrial Classification (SIC) codes and by corporation size within that code. To find the code in which your corporation is classified, use the index provided in the source. Some corporations are not easily categorized within a specific SIC. For example, the corporation may produce several products categorized in several industries. You may have to determine the industry that best fits your corporation.

Alternatively, you may want to compare your corporation to their closest competitor. Information concerning a primary competitor may be obtained in the annual report to stockholders or the Form 10-K of the competitor.

Mark the comparison method you will use:

☐   **Industry Comparison**

SIC Code: _____

Industry Name: _____

Source of industry-wide data: _____

All industry comparisons should be made using the same fiscal years. The most current year of operations may not yet be available in the industry source. What is the year of the comparison you will be making?

_____

☐   **Primary Competitor Comparison**

Name of Competitor: _____

In the following table, copy (1) common-size data and ratios calculated earlier for the appropriate year, and (2) the corresponding industry or comparison data. You may need to adjust certain ratios to make them comparable. For example, if the earnings before taxes are used to calculate return ratios for the industry, you should calculate your corporation's ratio in a similar manner. If the data is not available, indicate this by writing "NA" in the blank. (⌨ Competitor Analysis worksheet)

	Corporation	Industry or Competitor
Income Statement Common-Size Data		
Gross Profit/Sales	_____%	_____%
Income from Continuing Operations/Sales	_____%	_____%
Balance Sheet Common-Size Data		
Current Assets/Total Assets	_____%	_____%
Current Liabilities/Total Assets	_____%	_____%
Liabilities/Total Assets	_____%	_____%
Equity/Total Assets	_____%	_____%
Profitability Ratios		
Profit Margin	_____%	_____%
Return on Assets	_____%	_____%
Return on Equity	_____%	_____%
Dividend Payout Ratio	_____%	_____%
Liquidity Ratios		
Current Ratio	_____:1	_____:1
Quick Ratio	_____:1	_____:1
Solvency Ratios		
Liabilities/Total Assets	_____%	_____%
Times Interest Earned	_____times	_____times
Operational Ratios		
Inventory Turnover	_____times	_____times
Receivable Turnover	_____times	_____times

1. What are the primary differences between the corporation and other companies in the industry or the primary competitor? What factors explain the reasons for these differences?

_____

_____

_____

_____

_____

_____

_____

_____

_____

2. In your opinion, does the corporation compare favorably or unfavorably to the industry or the primary competitor? Give examples to support your conclusion.

_____

_____

_____

_____

_____

_____

_____

_____

_____

MAKING DECISIONS BASED ON THE ANNUAL REPORT

1. How would you assess the corporation's revenue and income performance over the last two years? What are the reasons for your assessment?

_____

_____

_____

_____

2. What factors (such as the economy, consumer demand, new products, competition, etc.) will have the greatest influence on in the determination of next year's revenue? In what way would these factor(s) influence revenue?

_____

_____

_____

_____

_____

3. What do you predict revenue to be next year? $ _____

4. What do you predict net income to be next year? $ _____

5. How would you assess the corporation's total asset growth rate (for example, rapid increase, stable increase, stagnant, declining)? What evidence justifies your answer?

_____

_____

_____

6. Do you expect total assets to increase decrease, or remain relatively the same next year? Justify your answer.

_____

_____

_____

_____

7. Do you believe the corporation will need additional financing to meet needs over the next few years? Why or why not? If financing is needed, do you believe the corporation would be able to obtain financing easily?

_____

_____

_____

_____

_____

_____

8. Identify what you believe to be the three strongest aspects of the corporation. Describe why these might be considered advantages.

a. _____

_____

b. _____

_____

c. _____

_____

9. Identify what you believe to be the three weakest aspects of the corporation. Is it likely these weaknesses can be overcome in the next few years?

a. _____

_____

b. _____

_____

c. _____

_____

10. Are you optimistic or pessimistic concerning the future of the corporation? What specific corporate or industry characteristics influence your opinion?

_____

_____

_____

_____

_____

11. Would you invest in the capital stock or bonds (if applicable) of this corporation if you had sufficient funds? Would you rather invest in one of the corporation's competitors? What are the reasons for your decision?

_____

_____

_____

_____

_____

APPENDIX A

HOW TO OBTAIN ANNUAL FINANCIAL DATA

Annual financial data of a corporation may be requested directly from the corporation or downloaded from the internet.

Requesting Financial Information Directly from the Corporation

Corporations are usually enthusiastic about complying with requests for annual reports. They know the recipient may be a potential stockholder in the corporation. Requests for an annual report or Form 10-K are usually fulfilled within two to three weeks.

You may request an annual report by letter or email. Annual reports may also be obtained by phoning shareholder service department of the corporation. Corporate addresses and phone numbers are usually easily found in a simple internet search. (🖰 in the corporate website search for stockholder, shareholder, or investor relations.) If you have difficulty finding an address on the internet, the following directories, which are available in most libraries, will be helpful:

Directory of Corporate Affiliations, National Register Publishing Co., Skokie, IL
Standard & Poor's register of corporations, directors and executives, Standard & Poor's, New York, NY
Thomas Register of American Manufacturers, Thomas Publishing Co., New York, NY
The ValueLine Investment Survey, A. Bernhard., New York, NY
Ward's Business Directory of U.S. Private and Public Companies, Gale Research, Detroit, MI

Caution: Some companies provide a "summary annual report" which includes the primary financial statements and summarized notes. They usually reference Form 10-K if the reader wants greater detail. Summarized annual reports alone do not contain adequate data to complete this project.

Downloading Financial Data from the Internet

Financial data of publicly-traded corporations are available on the corporate website and on the SEC website.

Corporate Website Almost every publicly-traded corporation now places annual financial data on their corporate website. The data may be (1) summarized from the corporate annual report, (2) the annual report submitted to stockholders, or (3) a link to documents submitted to the SEC. Annual financial data is usually located in the investor relations section of a corporate web site (🖰 stockholder, shareholder, or investor relations). The financial statements usually appear in either in a web-based format or a portable document format (pdf) file.

SEC Website The annual report submitted to the SEC is called Form 10-K. This form is publicly available on the internet (www.sec.gov) in a database called the Electronic Data Gathering, Analysis, and Retrieval system (EDGAR). A tutorial on accessing EDGAR is at www.sec.gov/edgar/quickedgar.htm.

Caution: Information downloaded from the internet may be obtained immediately; however, it is not always in a format that is easy to use. Printing the data is sometimes cumbersome.

APPENDIX B

OBTAINING INFORMATION FOR INDUSTRY COMPARISONS

The following publications are sources of industry-wide data available in most public and academic libraries:

Almanac of Business and Industrial Financial Ratios, Troy, Leo, Prentice Hall, Upper Saddle River, NJ
Annual Statement Studies, Robert Morris Associates, Philadelphia, PA
Industry Norms and Key Business Ratios, Dun and Bradstreet Credit Services, Inc., Murray Hill, NJ

Most industry comparison services organize data by Standard Industrial Classification (SIC) codes. If you have difficulty determining the SIC code for your corporation, refer to Occupational Safety and Health Administration's Standard Industrial Code Search on the internet at www.osha.gov/oshstats/sicser.html. If your corporation's securities are registered with the SEC, the primary SIC code(s) will be listed in Form 10-K located on the internet at www.sec.gov.

Some services also provide data for several corporate size categories (usually determined by revenue or total assets). Use the most appropriate industry and size for the corporation you selected.

APPENDIX C

FINANCIAL ANALYSIS USING EXCEL

To help you with this project, an Excel spreadsheet may be downloaded from www.mhhe.com/pasewark5e. The file contains four linked worksheets: Ratio Analysis, Competitor Analysis, Trend Analysis, and Seasonality. The spreadsheet may be completed in only a few minutes using data that you have already utilized in the project. The spreadsheet will also calculate ratios that will confirm calculations you made in the project.

Common Size and Ratio Analysis - On the Ratio Analysis worksheet, enter data in the cells with white backgrounds. As you enter the data, common-size data will appear in Columns C and E. Ratios will be calculated in Rows 41 through 61. The example shows data from ExxonMobil for the years 1997 through 2001.

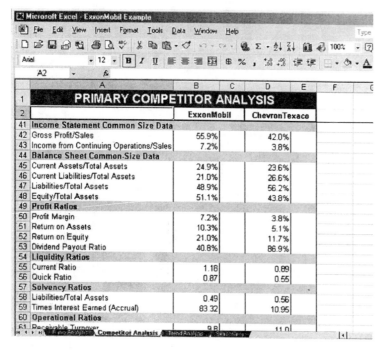

Competitor Analysis – Access the Competitor Analysis worksheet by clicking the Competitor Analysis tab at the bottom of the screen. The company data you entered on the Ratio Analysis worksheet is linked to the Competitor Analysis worksheet and need not be entered. Enter data for the company's primary competitor in the cells with white backgrounds on the Competitor Analysis worksheet. Comparative ratios will appear in Rows 41 through 62. The example shows comparative ratios calculated for ExxonMobil and ChevronTexaco.

48

Trend Analysis – The Trend Analysis worksheet summarizes the revenue, income, and total assets of the corporation for the last few years. All data on this sheet is linked to prior worksheets and need not be entered. The sheet will display column and line charts that indicate historical trends. The example shows a column chart of ExxonMobil revenue.

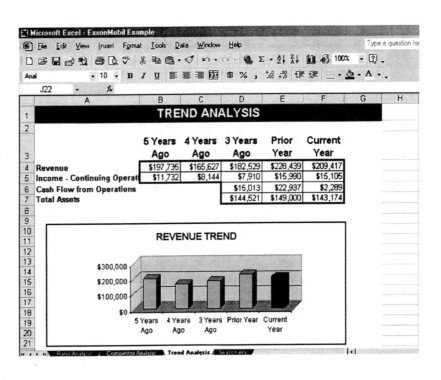

Seasonality – The last worksheet summarizes quarterly revenue, income, and stock prices. Enter quarterly data for the company in B4:E7 and B13:E14. Charts will be created in Rows 16 through 52 that indicate the seasonal trends of the revenue, income, and stock prices. The example shows a line chart created from the quarterly revenue of ExxonMobil.

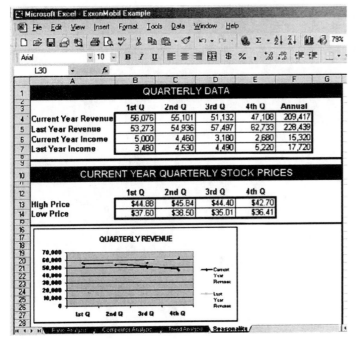